JINGLE BELL JOKES FOR FUNNY KIDS

RP|KIDS

PHILADELPHIA

Illustrated by
Andrew Pinder

Copyright © 2024 by Buster Books
Cover copyright © 2025 by Hachette Book Group, Inc.

Hachette Book Group supports the right to free expression and the value
of copyright. The purpose of copyright is to encourage writers and artists
to produce the creative works that enrich our culture.

The scanning, uploading, and distribution of this book without permission
is a theft of the author's intellectual property. If you would like permission
to use material from the book (other than for review purposes), please contact
permissions@hbgusa.com. Thank you for your support of the author's rights.

Running Press Kids
Hachette Book Group
1290 Avenue of the Americas, New York, NY 10104
www.runningpresskids.com
@runningpresskids

Originally published in 2024 by Buster Books,
an imprint of Michael O'Mara Books Limited, in Great Britain
First U.S. Edition: October 2025

Published by Running Press Kids, an imprint of Hachette Book Group, Inc.
The Running Press Kids name and logo are trademarks of Hachette Book Group, Inc.

The Hachette Speakers Bureau provides a wide range of authors
for speaking events. To find out more, go to www.hachettespeakersbureau.com
or email HachetteSpeakers@hbgusa.com.

Running Press books may be purchased in bulk for business, educational, or
promotional use. For more information, please contact your local bookseller or the
Hachette Book Group Special Markets Department at Special.Markets@hbgusa.com.

The publisher is not responsible for websites (or their content)
that are not owned by the publisher.

Text compiled and edited by Gary Panton
Print book cover design by Angie Allison
Interior design by Janene Spencer

Library of Congress Control Number: 2024949573

ISBNs: 979-8-89414-047-6 (paperback), 979-8-89414-048-3 (ebook)

Printed in Indiana, USA

LSC-C

Printing 2, 2025

CONTENTS

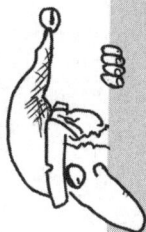

Introduction

**What did the snowman
say to the carrot?**

"Get out of my face!"

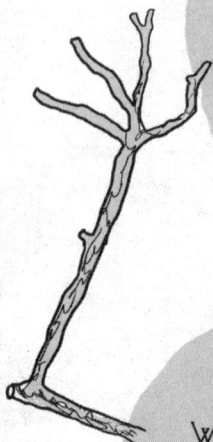

Welcome to this ho ho ho-larious
collection of jokes for funny kids.

In this book you will find more than
300 festive funnies that will have you
laughing your Christmas stockings off—from
wintery wisecracks to Santa banter.

If these Christmas jokes don't tickle
your funny bone, then nothing will. Don't
forget to share your favorites with your
friends and family over the holidays and
have them howling with laughter, too!

**What do Santa's helpers
use to bake cakes?**

Elf-raising flour.

**Why did the turkey
join the pop group?**

It was the only one
with drumsticks.

**What's invisible and smells
like milk and cookies?**

Santa's burps.

What's the best thing to put in a Christmas cake?

Your teeth.

What did one cranberry say to the other cranberry?

"'Tis the season to be jelly."

Why shouldn't you invite a turkey to spend Christmas with your family?

Because it uses fowl language.

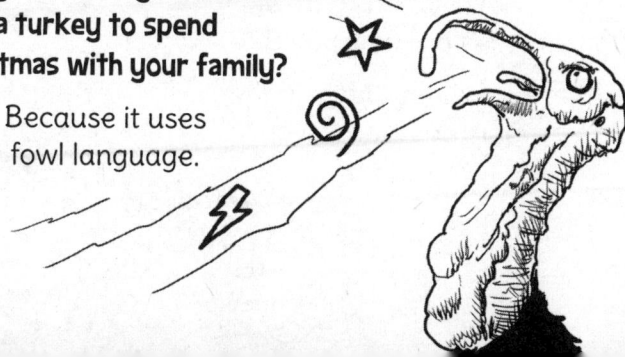

3

What did the turkey say to the hunter at Christmas?

"Quack, quack!"

Who lives in the jungle and swings from Christmas cake to Christmas cake?

Tarzipan.

What does Good King Wenceslas say when he's ordering pizza?

"Please can I have it deep pan, crisp, and even."

What's the most common Christmas whine?

"Oh no, I hate Brussels sprouts!"

What does Santa's mom put in his lunchbox?

Ho-ho-homemade cookies.

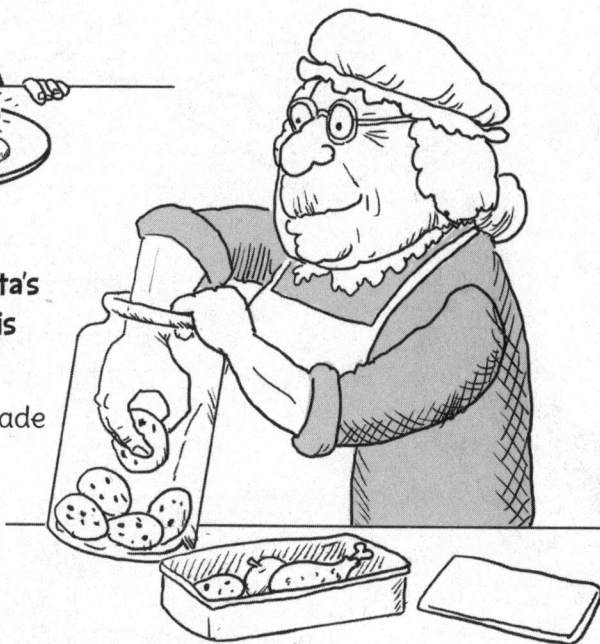

Why is a Christmas turkey never hungry?

Because it's stuffed.

What do elves eat for breakfast?

Mistle-toast.

Why did the turkey blush?

Because it saw the cranberry dressing.

What's red, white, and blue at Christmas?

A sad candy cane.

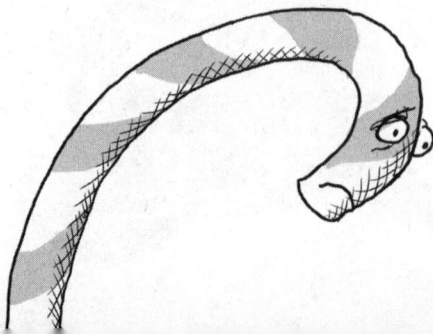

When is the only time it's okay to find a nose in your salad?

When it's a snowman's nose.

What kind of sweet treat does Rudolph love to eat?

Doe-nuts.

Why did the turkey cross the road?

Because it wasn't chicken.

**What do you call
a Christmas cake
with a bad cold?**

Coughy cake.

**What did the doctor
ask the gingerbread
man who hurt his ankle?**

"Have you tried icing it?"

**What kind of key
should you always
have at Christmas?**

A coo-key.

Did you hear about the Christmas pudding thief?

He was placed into custardy.

How do you know when a Christmas cake is feeling sad?

It's in tiers.

What kind of bread do elves like best?

Shortbread.

9

Why do people decorate the top of a Christmas cake?

Because it's too difficult to decorate the bottom.

If fruit comes from a fruit tree, where do turkeys come from?

A poul-tree.

What do gingerbread men use when they break their legs?

Candy canes.

How does Darth Vader like his Christmas turkey?

On the dark side.

What do polar bears eat for breakfast?

Frosted Flakes.

SILLY SNOWMEN

What was the snowman doing in the vegetable garden?

Picking his nose.

How do snowmen get home?

By riding an icicle.

Why did the snowman go to the doctor?

He was getting chills.

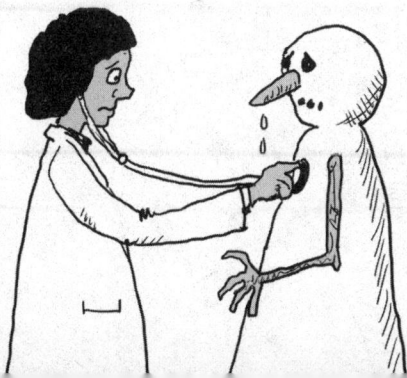

13

Where do snowmen dance?

At the snow ball.

Why did the snowman receive a certificate?

Because he was outstanding in his field.

What do snowmen eat for breakfast?

Ice crispies.

What happens when snowmen get angry?

They have a meltdown.

What did one snowman say to the other snowman?

"Can you smell carrots?"

What did the snowman order from the Mexican restaurant?

Brrrr-itos.

15

How do snowmen greet each other?

"Ice to see you."

What do you call a snowman driving a car?

A snowmobile.

What do you call a snowman in the summertime?

A puddle.

**How do you know
if a snowman is
unhappy with you?**

He'll give you the
cold shoulder.

**Did you hear about
the snowman spy?**

He has a license to chill.

**What do you call a
snowman's dandruff?**

Snowflakes.

17

What movie do snowmen love?

Snow White.

How do snowmen find out what the weather's going to be like?

They look on the winternet.

M	T	W	T	F	S	S

Why is Frosty never late?

Because time waits for snowman.

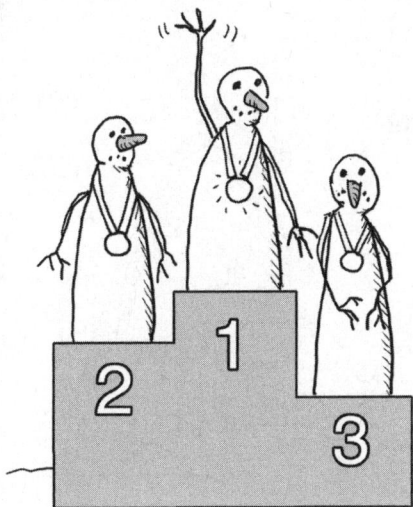

What do snowmen win at the Olympics?

Cold medals.

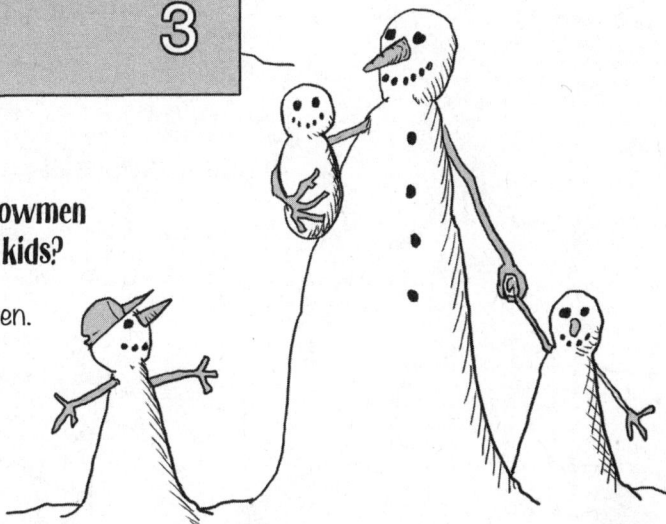

What do snowmen call their kids?

Chill-dren.

What did the police officer say when she caught a snowman stealing?

"Freeze!"

What do you call a snowman who loves to bake cakes?

Frosty the dough-man.

How do snowmen lose weight?

They wait for the weather to get warmer.

What did the snowman say to the carrot?

"Get out of my face!"

CLAUS GUFFAWS

What's it called when
Santa takes a break?

A Santa pause.

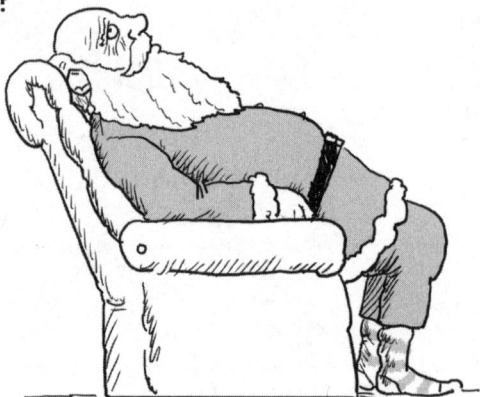

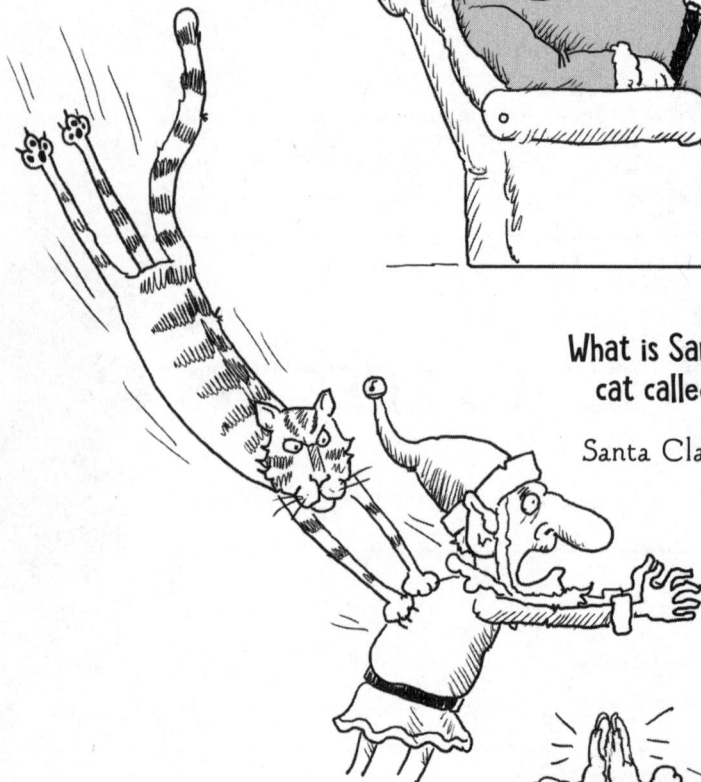

What is Santa's
cat called?

Santa Claws.

What's it called when
Santa claps his hands?

Santapplause.

22

What do you call Santa
when he's on the beach?

Sandy Claus.

Who brings fizzy orange soda
to children at Christmas?

Fanta Claus.

What's it called when
Santa warms himself
by the fire?

Santa Thaws.

23

How does Santa do the gardening?

With a hoe hoe hoe.

How does Santa pay for his electricity?

Jingle bills.

What do you get if you leave the fire lit and Santa comes down the chimney?

Crisp Kringle.

Why does Santa hate cramped spaces?

He suffers from Claus-trophobia.

Santa: Doctor, Doctor! I have a pie stuck to my bottom!

Doctor: Don't worry, I have some cream for that.

Where does Santa go for his swimming lessons?

The North Pool.

25

What kind of motorcycle
does Santa have?

A Holly Davidson.

What did the naughty sports
commentator get from Santa?

COOOOOOOAAAAAALLLLLL!

Who is Santa's most
chilled-out friend?

Jack Frost.

What's red and white and
falls down a chimney?

Santa Klutz.

What language does
Santa speak?

North Polish.

Why does Santa wear red
to climb down chimneys?

Because it soots him.

How does Santa wash his hands?

With hand Santa-tizer.

How much did Santa pay for his sleigh?

Nothing—it was on the house.

What's red and white and solves mysteries?

Santa Clues.

What do you call Santa when he's in the South Pole?

A lost Claus.

What kind of car does Santa drive?

A Toy-ota.

What do you say if Santa's taking the school attendance?

"Present."

29

What's red and white
and goes, "Oh oh oh"?

Santa walking
backward.

What goes, "Ho ho WHOOSH!
Ho ho WHOOSH!"?

Santa walking through
a revolving door.

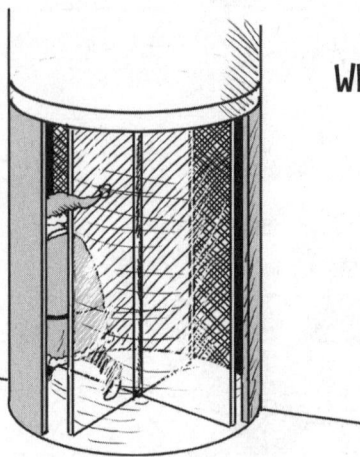

What goes,
"Ho ho THUMP"?

Santa laughing
his head off.

Which state does Santa like best?

Ida-ho-ho-ho.

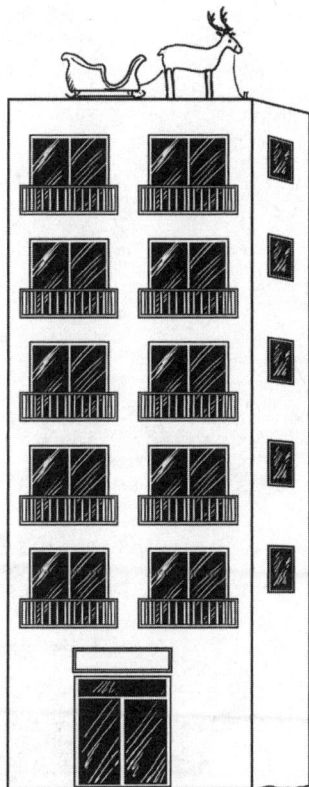

Where does Santa go when he's on vacation?

To a ho-ho-hotel.

31

Why does Santa like thinking about last Christmas?

He's Santa-mental.

How did Santa propose to Mrs. Claus?

"Will you merry me?"

What's the difference between Santa and a dog?

One wears a red suit, and the other just pants.

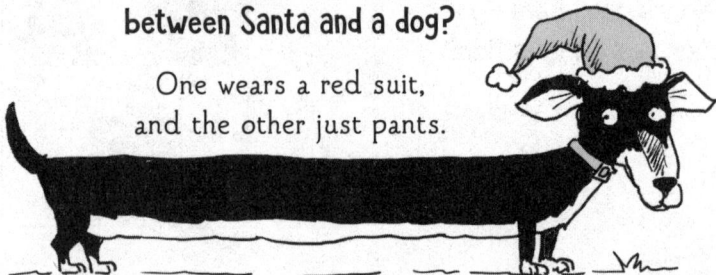

How do you know that Santa
is good at karate?

He wears a black belt.

What do you call Santa
when he forgets to put on
his underwear?

St. Knickerless.

Who does Santa call when
his sleigh breaks down?

The abominable towman.

KNOCK, KNOCK!

Knock, knock!

Who's there?

Noah.

Noah who?

Noah-ny good Christmas jokes?

Knock, knock!

Who's there?

Mary.

Mary who?

Mary Christmas and a Happy New Year!

Knock, knock!

Who's there?

Way.

Way who?

Way-k me up once Santa's come.

Knock, knock!

Who's there?

Dexter.

Dexter who?

Dexter halls with boughs of holly, Fa-la-la-la-la, la-la-la-la!

Knock, knock!

Who's there?

Holly.

Holly who?

Holly-days are coming!

Knock, knock!

Who's there?

Interrupting Santa.

Interr–

HO HO HO!

Knock, knock!

Who's there?

Honda.

Honda who?

**Honda twelfth day of Christmas
my true love gave to me,
Twelve drummers drumming,
Eleven pipers piping,
Ten lords a-leaping,
Nine ladies dancing,
Eight maids a-milking,
Seven swans a-swimming,
Six geese a-laying,
Fiiiiiive goooooollld rings,
Four calling birds,
Three French hens,
Two turtle doves,
And a partridge in a pear tree!**

Knock, knock!

Who's there?

Santa.

Santa who?

**Santa Christmas
card to you,
did you get it yet?**

Knock, knock!

Who's there?

Justin.

Justin who?

**Justin time for
Christmas dessert!**

Knock, knock!

Who's there?

Coal.

Coal who?

**Coal me if you hear
Santa coming.**

Knock, knock!

Who's there?

Gladys.

Gladys who?

Gladys Christmas, it's the best time of year!

Knock, knock!

Who's there?

Avery.

Avery who?

Avery merry Christmas to you!

Knock, knock!

Who's there?

Radio.

Radio who?

Radio-r not, it's Christmas!

Knock, knock!

Who's there?

Dewey.

Dewey who?

Dewey know when Santa's going to arrive?

Knock, knock!

Who's there?

Scold.

Scold who?

Scold enough to go ice-skating.

Knock, knock!

Who's there?

Philip.

Philip who?

**Philip my stocking
with presents, please.**

Knock, knock!

Who's there?

Donut.

Donut who?

**Donut open this present
until Christmas.**

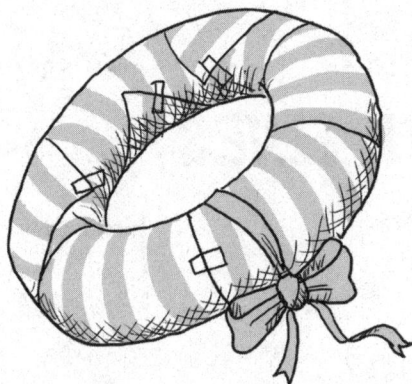

Knock, knock!

Who's there?

Ho ho.

Ho ho who?

**Your Santa impression
needs a little work.**

EXCELLENT ELVES

What does Santa do when the elves misbehave?

He gives them the sack.

What do Santa's little helpers learn at school?

The elf-abet.

What do Santa's little helpers do when they get home from school?

Their gnomework.

43

Where do Santa's little helpers go when they feel sick?

The elf clinic.

Why are Santa's little helpers so good at making toys?

They're elf-taught.

What do you call an elf with lots of money?

Welfy.

What kind of photos do
Santa's little helpers
love to take?

Elfies.

Why was Santa's little
helper feeling sad?

Because he had
low elf-esteem.

What do you call an
elf who won't share?

Elfish.

45

What sport do elves do best?

North Pole-vaulting.

Why did the elf go to sleep in the forest?

Because she wanted to sleep like a log.

Where do elves go to launch their movie careers?

Holly-wood.

Why did Santa's little helper go to the hospital?

To be nursed back to elf.

What do Santa's little helpers like to eat for lunch?

Elf-abetti spaghetti.

Why do Santa's little helpers wear hard hats in the toy factory?

For elf and safety.

**Where is the best place
to find elves?**

Wherever you
left them.

**How long should
an elf's legs be?**

Just long enough to
reach the ground.

What do elves say when they bump into each other?

"Small world, isn't it?"

Which one of Santa's little helpers can carry the most books?

The booksh-elf.

Why are there so many fruits and vegetables in Santa's workshop?

To promote elf-y eating.

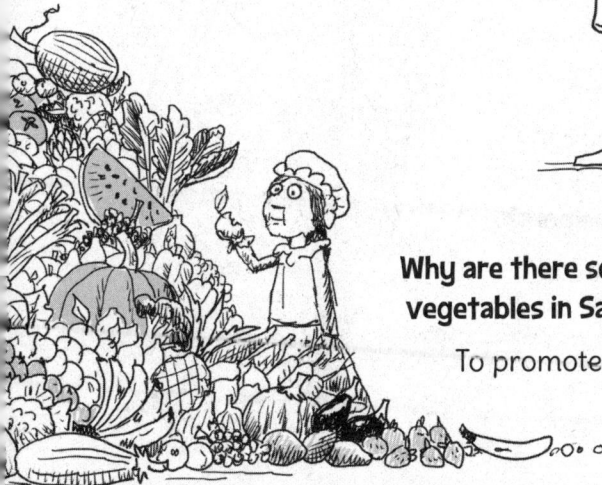

Where do elves go to vote?

The North Poll.

If athletes get athlete's foot, what do elves get?

Mistle-toes.

What do you call someone who works for Santa's little helpers?

Elf-employed.

BRRRR!

Why is it always cold at Christmas?

Because it's Decem-brrrr.

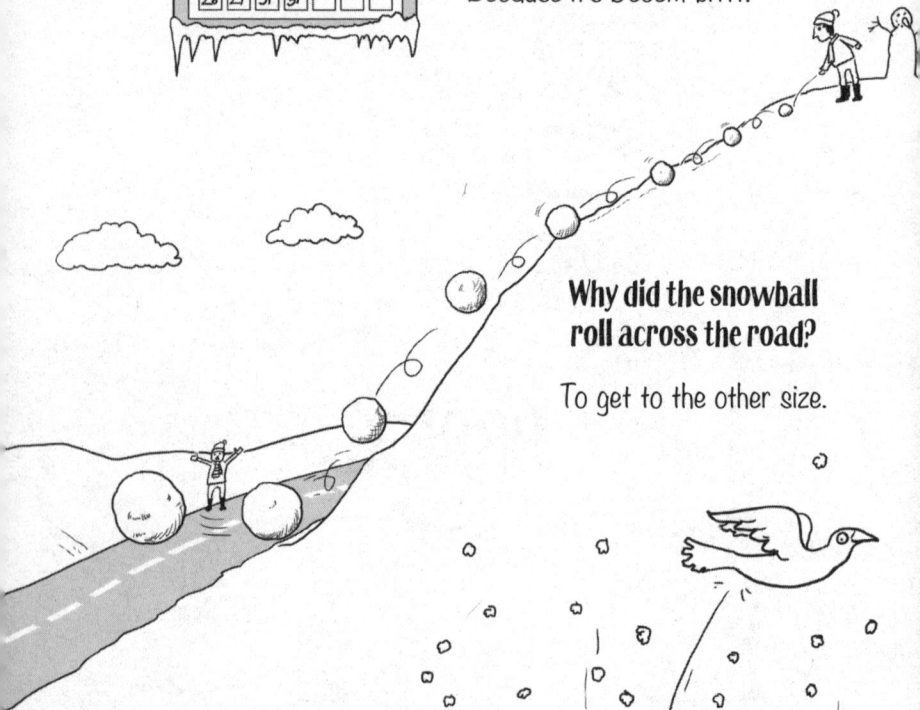

Why did the snowball roll across the road?

To get to the other size.

What's a good Christmas tip?

Never catch snowflakes on your tongue until all the birds have flown south for the winter.

What kind of painting looks best in the snow?

An elf-portrait.

What did the hat say to the scarf?

"You hang around here while I go on ahead."

Why should you never laugh about being buried in snow?

Because it's snow joke.

53

Why does your nose get tired in winter?

It spends all day running.

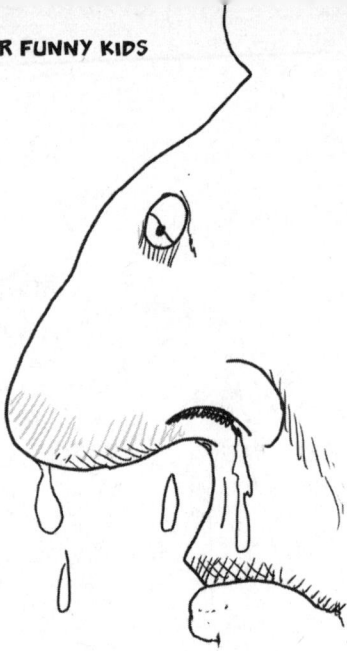

What did the icy road say to the car?

"Want to go for a spin?"

Why did the skiing instructor hate her job?

It went downhill fast.

Why did Princess Elsa fall off her sled?

She let it go.

How does a snowy Christmas day always end?

With a letter "y."

What falls and never gets hurt?

Snow.

55

What do you call a warm, red sock that won't leave you alone?

A Christmas stalking.

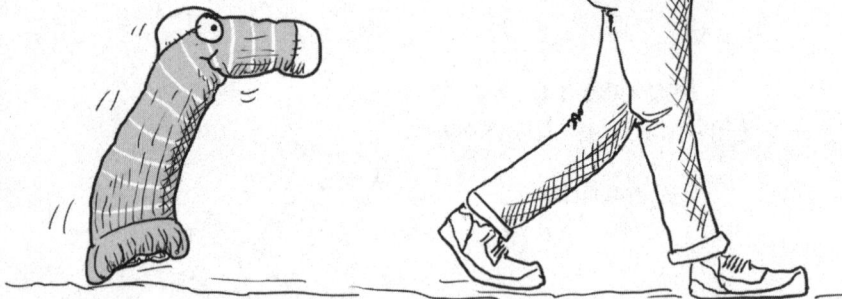

Why did the Christmas sweater become a comedian?

It had everyone in stitches.

**When is a boat
just like snow?**

When it's adrift.

**What did the snowman
say to the snowflake?**

"You're one of a kind."

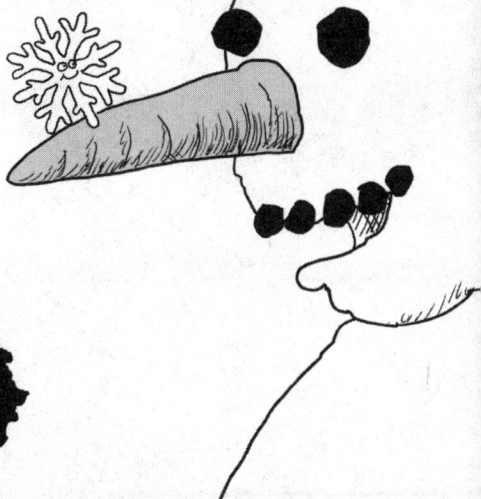

**What kind of ball can you
throw, but never bounce?**

A snowball.

A VERY SPOOKY CHRISTMAS

Why couldn't the
skeleton go to the
Christmas party?

It had no-body
to go with.

What do you get if you cross
a vampire with a snowman?

Frostbite.

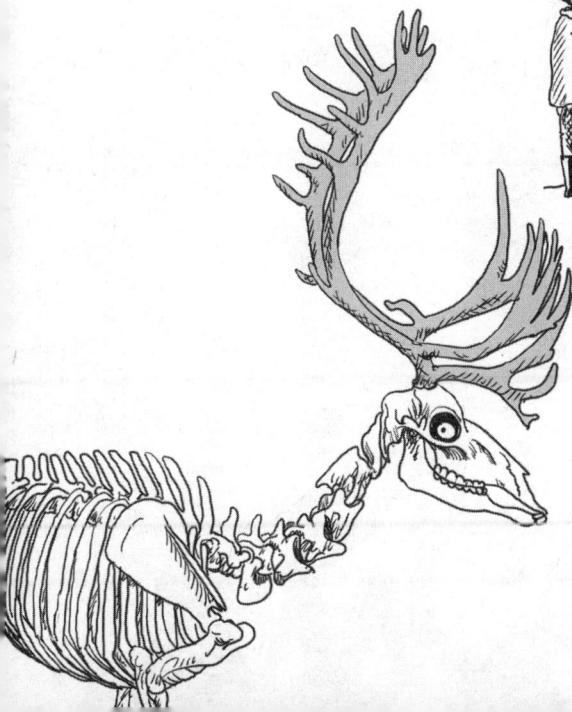

What do you call a
reindeer's ghost?

A cari-BOO!

What do ghosts put on
their Christmas dinner?

Grave-y.

How did Scrooge
score a goal?

The ghost of
Christmas passed.

What do vampires sing
on New Year's Eve?

Auld Fang Syne.

What kind of plates do skeletons
serve their Christmas dinner on?

Bone china.

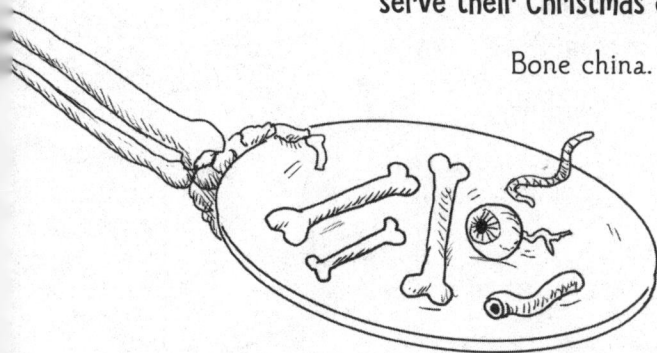

What do you call the
ghost of a turkey?

A poultry-geist.

Why did the mummy
spend Christmas alone?

He was too wrapped
up in himself.

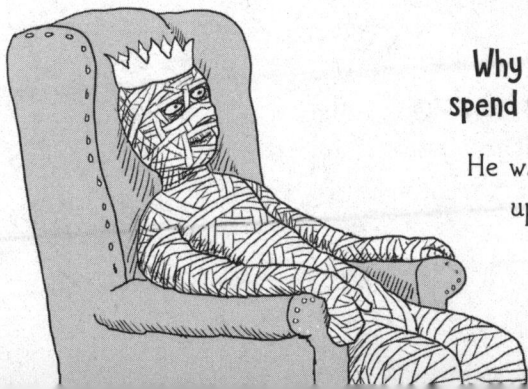

Why do mummies like giving
Christmas presents?

They're great at wrapping.

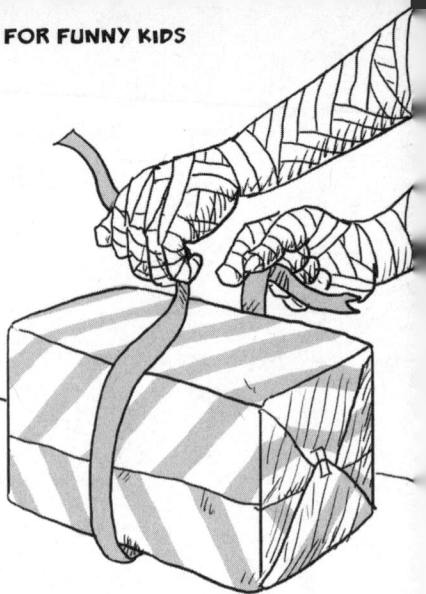

What do you call a yeti
with a six-pack?

The abdominal snowman.

Why did the cyclops go sking
instead of skiing?

Because it only had one "i."

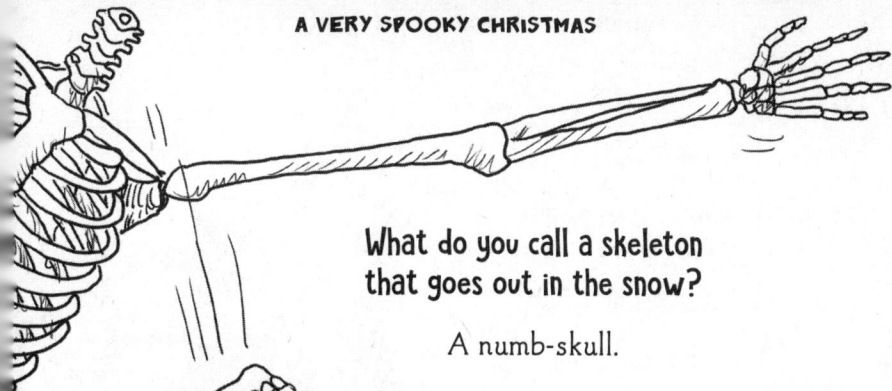

What do you call a skeleton that goes out in the snow?

A numb-skull.

Why do ghosts make great Christmas guests?

They always get into the festive spirit.

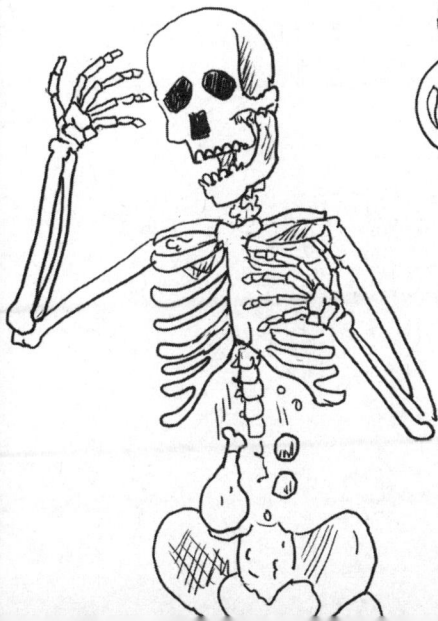

Why was the skeleton scared of eating Christmas dinner?

It didn't have the guts.

What do vampires celebrate in the month before Christmas?

Fangs-giving.

Where do ghosts buy their Christmas presents from?

BOO-tiques.

Where do zombies spend their Christmas vacation?

The Dead Sea.

What do ghosts have for Christmas dinner?

I-scream.

Why did the ghost's Christmas party get canceled?

Because people were dying to get in.

CANCELED

What bites but has no teeth?

Frost.

How do vampires start
their letters to Santa?

"Tomb it may concern..."

What did the three
monsters give as
Christmas presents?

Gold, Frankenstein,
and myrrh.

TREE-MENDOUS

**Why can't
Christmas trees knit?**

Because they keep
dropping their needles.

**Why did the Christmas
tree go for a haircut?**

It needed a trim.

What school subject did Santa like best?

Chemis-tree.

What did the Christmas tree do when its bank closed?

It started its own branch.

What do you get if you eat a Christmas tree?

Tinsel-itis.

What happens to Christmas trees if you stand still for too long?

They get pins and needles.

Why did the Christmas tree fail its exam?

The questions had it stumped.

Where do young trees go to learn how to be Christmas trees?

Elemen-tree school.

What looks like half a Christmas tree?

The other half.

What do Christmas trees wear to go swimming?

Trunks.

What did the beaver say to the Christmas tree?

"Nice gnawing you."

Why do Christmas trees all live in the past?

Because the present's beneath them.

What do you get when you cross a Christmas tree with an iPhone?

A pineapple.

What did one Christmas tree say to the other Christmas tree?

"Lighten up!"

What month do Christmas trees hate the most?

Sep-timber.

What do reindeer use to decorate their Christmas trees?

Hornaments.

What candy do Christmas trees like best?

Orna-mints.

How do Christmas trees check their email?

They log on.

Why did the Christmas tree go to the dentist?

It needed a root canal.

How do Christmas trees get ready for a party?

They spruce themselves up.

REINDEER RIB-TICKLERS

Why did Rudolph have to retake his exam?

Because he went down in history.

What did Santa say to Mrs. Claus when he stepped in a puddle?

"It must have reindeer."

How do Dasher, Prancer, and Dancer know when Christmas is coming?

They check their calen-deers.

Why did no one want to buy Donner and Blitzen?

Because they were two deer.

What did Rudolph say before he told a joke?

"This one will sleigh you!"

Why did the reindeer help an old lady cross the road?

It would have been Rudolph him not to.

77

Why does Scrooge have his own herd of reindeer?

So he can count his bucks.

What does Rudolph say to Santa when the sleigh takes off?

"Hold on for deer life."

What's the difference between a knight and a reindeer?

One slays a dragon; the other drags a sleigh.

What do you call a reindeer with no eyes?

No eye deer.

What do you call a reindeer with no eyes and no legs?

Still no eye deer.

What do you call a reindeer with three eyes?

A reiiindeer.

79

What do Santa's reindeer play at sleepovers?

Truth or deer.

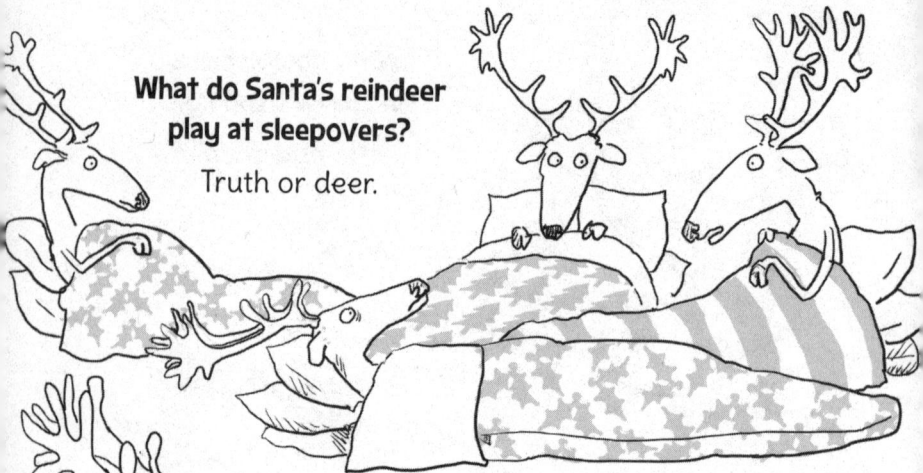

Where does Rudolph get all his celebrity gossip from?

Stag-azines.

What did Prancer say to Dancer?

"You're my deer-est pal."

What do you call a reindeer dressed as a pirate?

A buck-aneer.

What do you call a reindeer with bad manners?

Rude-olph.

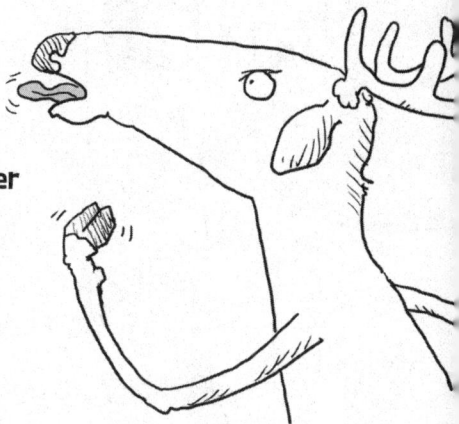

Why did Rudolph set up his own business?

To make some doe.

81

Who visits Rudolph and leaves money under his pillow?

The hoof fairy.

Why should you not write a book on reindeer?

Because writing a book on paper is easier.

Who is Santa's meanest reindeer?

Olive, because "Olive the other reindeer, used to laugh and call him names…"

CHRISTMAS CREATURES

What's green, covered in bulbs, and goes "ribbit"?

A mistle-toad.

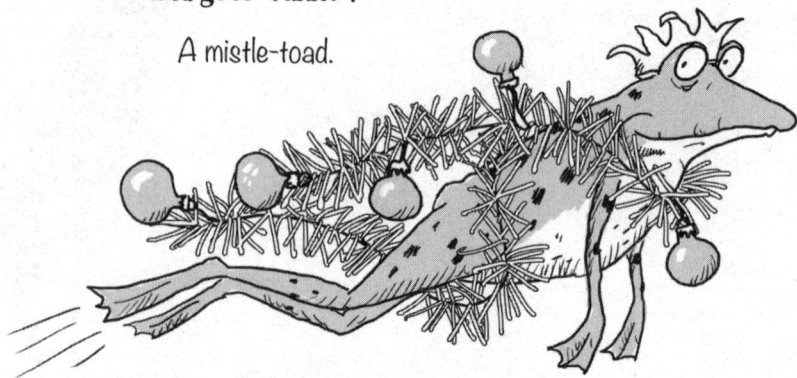

Who do sharks write letters to at Christmas?

Santa Jaws.

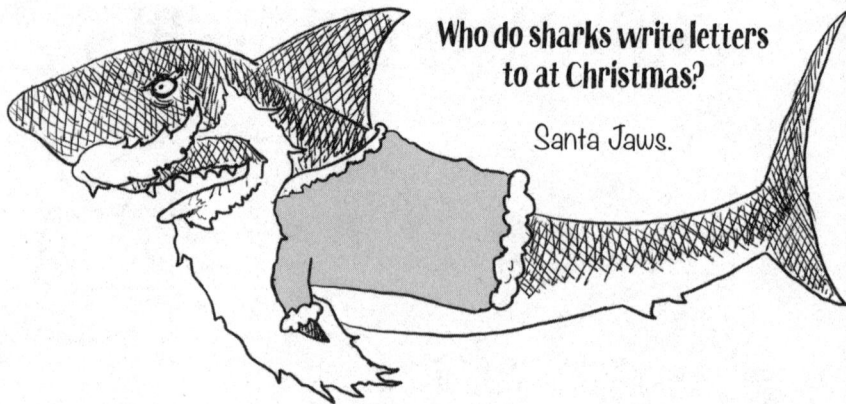

Why don't penguins and polar bears get along?

Because they're polar opposites.

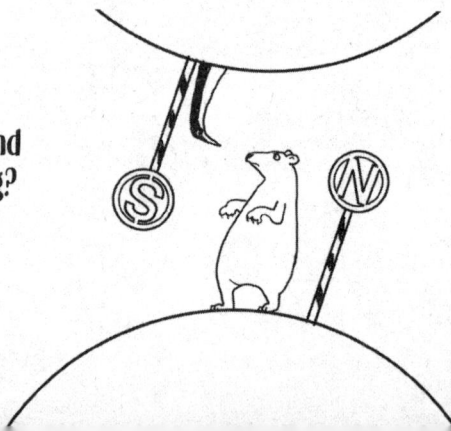

What do monkeys sing at Christmas?

"Jungle bells, jungle bells, jungle all the way!"

What do you call a polar bear wearing ear muffs?

Anything you want, he can't hear you.

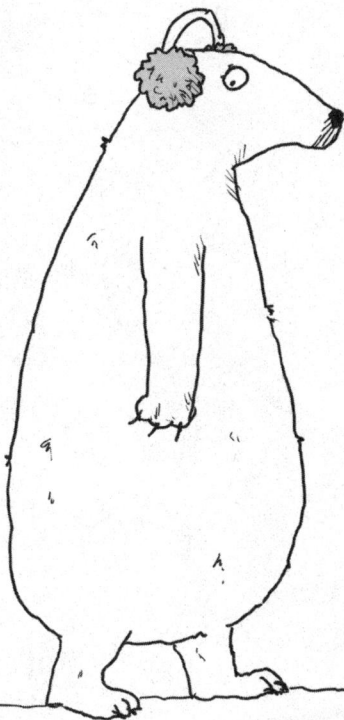

What do you call a chicken in the North Pole?

Lost.

What do you call a polar bear with no teeth?

A gummy bear.

What do sheep say to each other on Christmas morning?

"Fleece Navidad!"

What do cats say to each other at Christmas?

"Meowy Christmas and a Happy Mew Year!"

What do angry mice send to each other at Christmas?

Cross-mouse cards.

What do penguins wear on their feet when they're at home?

Slippers.

What's white, furry, and tastes of chocolate and caramel?

A rolo bear.

Why don't polar bears wear shoes?

They prefer to have bear feet.

What does Scrooge's pet sheep say at Christmas?

"Baaaaah, humbug!"

What do skunks sing at Christmas?

Jingle Smells.

**Why do penguins
swim in salt water?**

Because pepper
makes them sneeze.

**What kind of key should you always
have in your nativity play?**

A don-key.

**What do you call a polar
bear caught in the rain?**

A drizzly bear.

What do penguins wear on their heads?

Ice caps.

What kind of bug hates Christmas?

A bah humbug.

What do polar bears do if they need to pee during a movie?

They press the paws button.

What do you call a dog made from snow?

A slush puppy.

What did the polar bear do when it felt too hot?

It turned up the bear conditioning.

What did the penguin say when it saw a flying reindeer?

Nothing. Penguins can't talk.

91

What kind of reptile loves snow?

A b-lizzard.

Which side of a polar bear has the most fur?

The outside.

How does a penguin build its house?

Igloos it together.

Why do birds fly south for winter?

Because it's too far to walk.

What do donkeys send each other at Christmas?

Mule-tide greetings.

What do you get if you cross a polar bear with a seal?

A polar bear.

MERRY MUSIC

What Christmas carol
do parents love?

"Silent Night."

Which singer do Santa's
little helpers like best?

Elvish Presley.

95

Which pop star does
Rudolph love to listen to?

Beyon-sleigh.

What do snowmen sing
at birthday parties?

"Freeze a Jolly
Good Fellow."

What Christmas carol
is sung in the desert?

"Oh, Camel Ye Faithful."

What did the wobbly dessert sing at Christmas?

"'Tis the Season to be Jello."

What Christmas carol do vegans love?

"Soy to the World."

What do you call a snowman who can play the piano?

Melton John.

What kind of music
do elves like best?

Wrap.

Which Christmas carol
do ducks like best?

"In the Beak Midwinter."

What should you sing if you
feel sick at Christmas?

"No-well, no-well."

Which singer do Christmas trees love to listen to?

Spruce Springsteen.

Which Christmas song does Santa like best?

"Have Your Elf a Merry Little Christmas."

What do fish sing at Christmas?

Christmas corals.

99

Which Christmas carol do dogs like best?

"Bark! The Herald Angels Sing."

What did the strawberry sing to the raspberry on Christmas morning?

"We Wish You a Berry Christmas."

GIFTING GIGGLES

Why is a broken drum the best Christmas present?

Because you can't beat it.

What did the Three Wise Men say after handing over the gold and frankincense?

"Wait, there's myrrh."

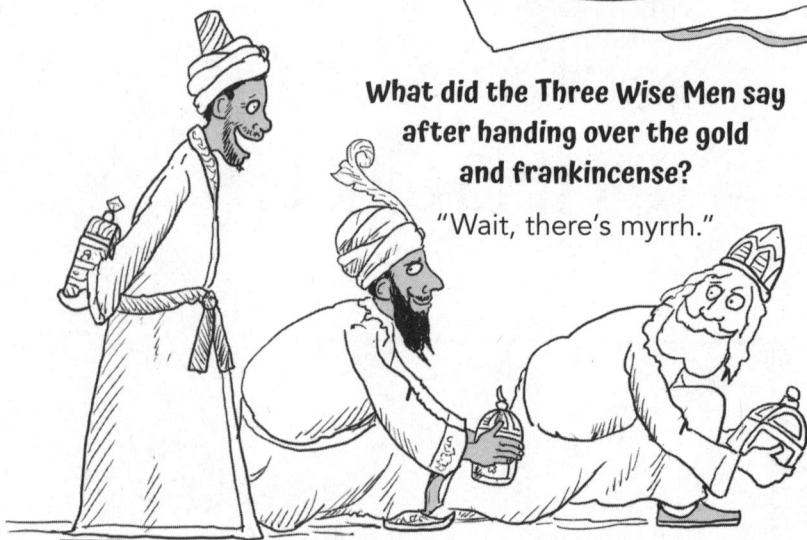

What did the farmer get for Christmas?

A cow-culator.

Why do sticky playing cards make a bad Christmas present?

Because they're very hard to deal with.

Who delivers Christmas presents to pets?

Santa Paws.

**How can you tell when
Santa has arrived
on your roof?**

You can just sense
his presents.

**Why don't shrimp give
Christmas presents?**

Because they're shellfish.

**Why do calendars make
bad Christmas presents?**

Because their days
are numbered.

Why was E the only letter in the alphabet to get a present from Santa?

Because the other letters were not-E.

ABC DFGHIJ

What did the Christmas card say to the stamp?

"Stick with me and we'll go places."

How did the snowglobe feel when it was given as a gift?

A little shaken.

What should you do if your new Christmas sweater gives you an electric shock?

Exchange it for another one, free of charge.

Why does a comb make a good Christmas present?

Because it's a parting gift.

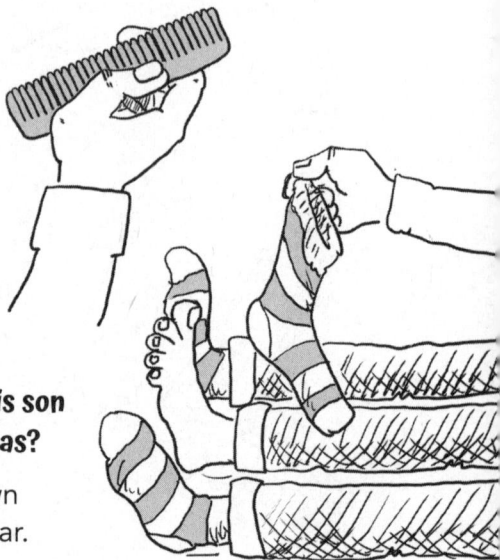

Why did the man buy his son one sock for Christmas?

Because he'd grown another foot this year.

**What do you call the
terms and conditions
on a Christmas present?**

The Santa clauses.

**Why didn't the shoelace get
any Christmas presents?**

Because it had been knotty.

**Why does a foot make a
good Christmas present?**

Because it's a stocking filler.

107

Why did the boy's mom get him a fridge for Christmas?

She wanted to see his face light up when he opened it.

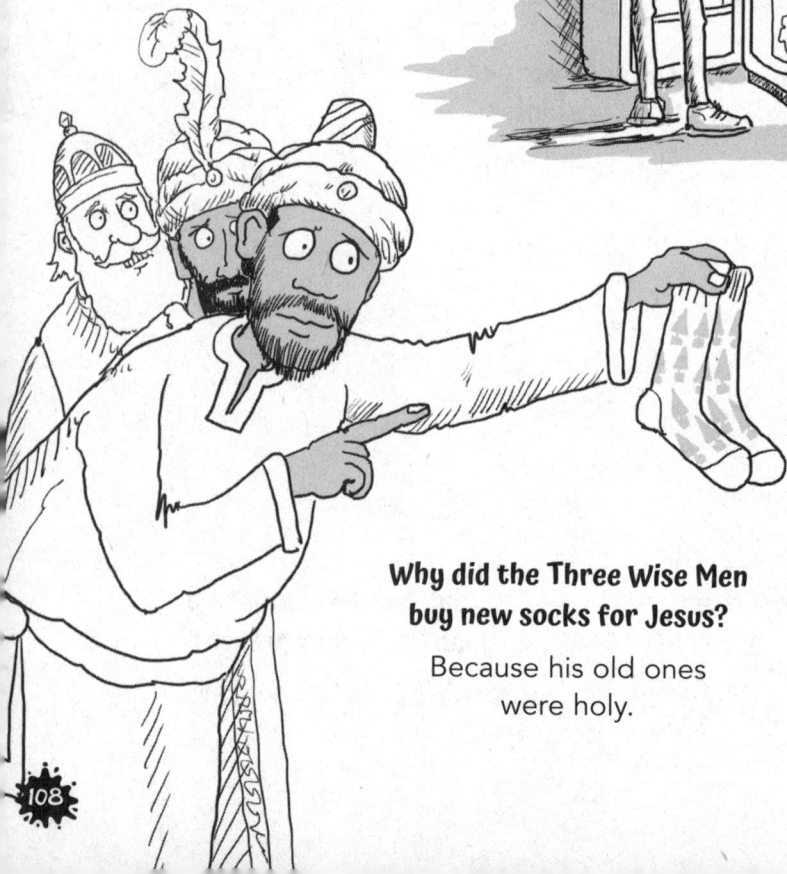

Why did the Three Wise Men buy new socks for Jesus?

Because his old ones were holy.

PARTY TIME

How did the chickens dance at the Christmas party?

Chick to chick.

What part of the body do you only see at Christmas parties?

The mistle-toe.

Why do snowmen make great party guests?

Because they're good at breaking the ice.

How do astronauts organize
their Christmas party?

They planet.

Why couldn't the shoelace
go to the Christmas party?

It was all tied up.

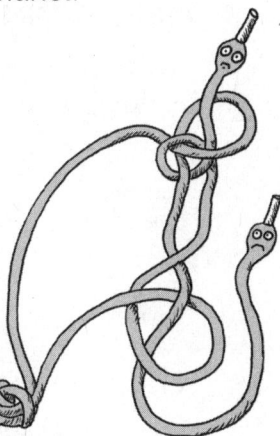

What did everyone sing at
the Christmas tree's party?

"Fir he's a jolly good fellow,
fir he's a jolly good fellow..."

Why didn't the snowman go to the Christmas party?

He had snowone to go with.

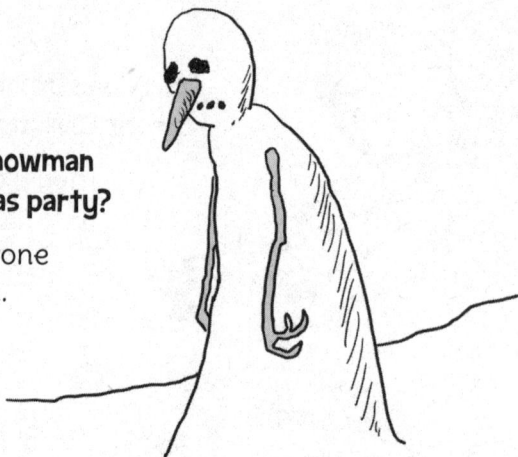

Did you hear about the werewolf's Christmas party?

It was a howling success.

Why didn't the cookie go to the Christmas party?

It was feeling crumbly.

Why did the math book look sad at the Christmas party?

Because it had a lot of problems.

Why did the mushroom get invited to lots of Christmas parties?

Because he was a fun-gi.

What snack did the snowman serve at his Christmas party?

Ice chips.

Why did Santa wear sunglasses to the Christmas party?

Because he didn't want to be recognized.

What did the candle say on the day of the Christmas party?

"I'm going out tonight."

Why was the broom late to the Christmas party?

It over-swept.

Who can you always find in the bathroom at Christmas parties?

The party pooper.

Why did the teddy bear stop eating the Christmas party food?

It was stuffed.

115

**What do penguins call
their Christmas party?**

The snow ball.

**Why did the cow go to
the Christmas party?**

To have an udderly
good time.

**Why did the singer bring a
ladder to the Christmas party?**

Because she wanted to
reach the high notes.

HAPPY NEW YEAR!

117

In what year does New Year's Day come before Christmas?

Every year.

What did the champagne bottle call his dad?

Pop!

What's a cow's favorite day of the year?

Moo Year's Eve.

What do pigs give each other on New Year's Eve?

Hogs and kisses.

What do ghosts say to each other on New Year's Day?

Happy Boo Year!

Knock, knock!

Who's there?

Abby.

Abby who?

Abby New Year!

What happened to the man who stole a calendar on New Year's Eve?

He got 12 months.

Why does bread hate New Year's Eve?

Because it always has to make a toast.

Why did the woman stand on one leg at midnight on New Year's Eve?

She wanted to start the year on the right foot.

What do rabbits say to each other on New Year's Day?

"Hoppy New Year!"

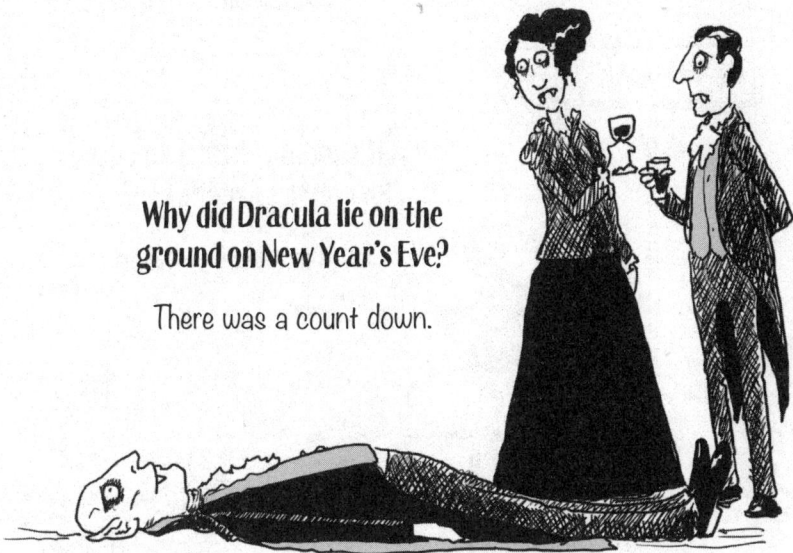

Why did Dracula lie on the ground on New Year's Eve?

There was a count down.

What do farmers grow on January 1st?

New Year's Hay.

What do wildebeest say to each other on New Year's Day?

"Happy Gnu Year!"

AULD L'ANG

What should you do if you get lost on New Year's Eve?

Follow the Auld Lang Sign.

What was Dr. Frankenstein's New Year's resolution?

To make some new friends.

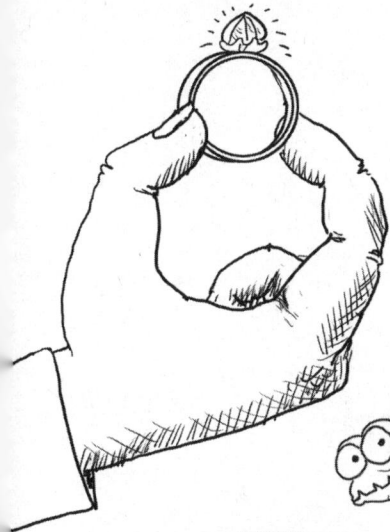

What do jewelers do on January 1st?

Ring in the New Year.

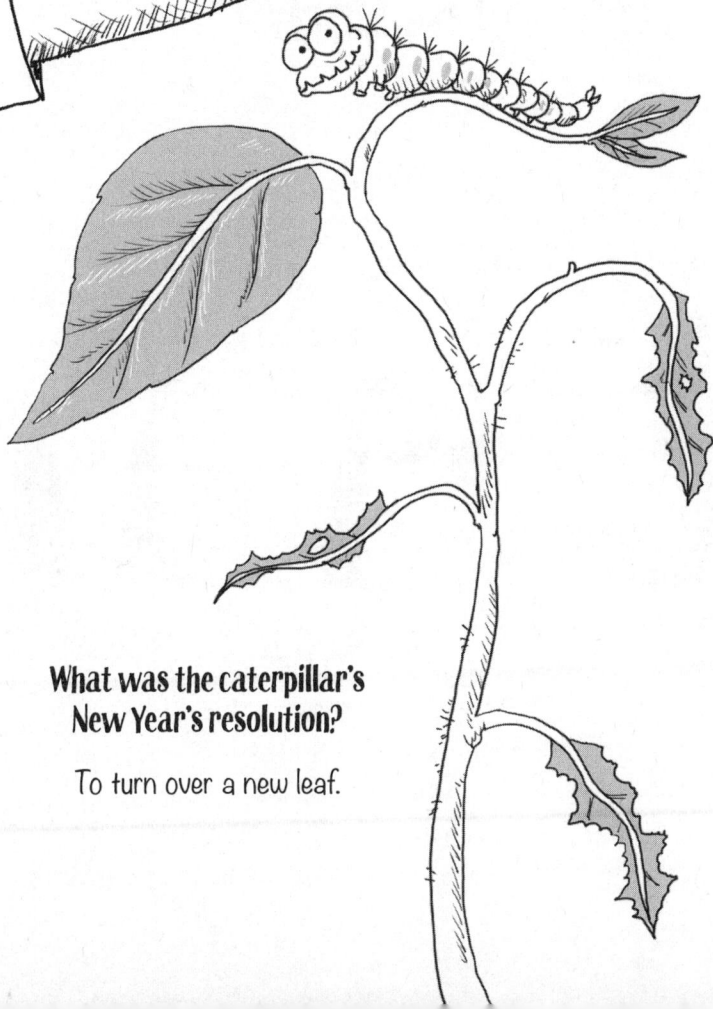

What was the caterpillar's New Year's resolution?

To turn over a new leaf.

123

The End